What Readers Are Saying About *Dear Author*

"Having known Laura as long as I have, I can say without a doubt she is the most encouraging person I know. With *Dear Author: Letters from a Bookish Fangirl*, she's channeled all her enthusiastic warmth into her work. It's the perfect way for her readers to carry a hug in your pocket."
—C. S. Johnson, award-winning author of The Order of the Crystal Daggers

"There's just nothing like this. Personalized, perfect encouragement for every single author out there. The types of letters you have received, or wish you could receive, that share the heart of every fan girl out there. The kind of thing you cry and cheer over and makes you keep going as an author. Laura A. Grace's special brand of encouragement is priceless."
—R.J. Conte, bestselling author of *Lucent Sylph*

"Being a writer can be a discouraging and lonely endeavor at times. Laura A. Grace's *Dear Author: Letters from a Bookish Fangirl* are notes full of encouragement and the reminders we need to keep creating. She helps us remember why we tell stories by connecting us with the joy of our readers like only a genuine fangirl can."
—Tabitha Caplinger, author of the Chronicle of the Three Trilogy

"This book is a perfect gift for the writers on your Christmas list!"
 —J.M. Hackman, author of the Firebrand Chronicles

Dear Author

Dear Author

Letters from a Bookish Fangirl

LAURA A. GRACE

© Copyright 2019 by Laura Pol

All rights reserved. No part of this publication may be reproduced, stored in a retrieval system, or transmitted in any form or by any means—for example electronic, photocopy, recording—without the prior written permission of the author. The only exception is brief quotations in printed reviews.

Published by Unicorn Quester Books, LLC
unicornquester.com

Artwork by Hannah S.J. Williams

ISBN: 9781733376808 (paperback)

Printed in the United States of America

Table of Contents

1	Introduction
5	Always Rereading
7	Character Conversations
9	Your Debut
13	You'll Publish Soon
15	Thank You
17	Release Day
21	I Can't Cope
23	It's Done?
25	I'm Here for You
29	I'm Not Afraid to Bribe
31	I See You
33	Recommending to Everyone
37	Rescue Your Characters
39	Thank You

41   Please Be You
45   Acknowledgements
48   About the Author

To the Inspirer of Words,
you make me brave.

Introduction

Dear Reader,

It hit me afresh when writing this book that words have power. That may not be surprising, as it's a seemingly small truth, yet it's one that carries consequences to sometimes extreme lengths. A word of affirmation from a loved one, a compliment from a stranger, or a small "well done" from a supervisor. A few simple words can transform a person's day in an instant.

Though not spoken, I realized written words woven together to create a story are a lot like that too. Within the course of a few paragraphs, a reader could be teleported to a fictional realm or alongside a detective, solving the next big mystery. (And that's just mentioning *two* different possibilities!) Imagine that reader continuing to read paragraph after paragraph, page after page. Those characters are now no longer just "characters"—they're friends. That fictional world is no longer just "fictional." It's a home-away-from-home.

I know this is not a fictitious outcome, or even an aspiring ideal, because my bookish life testifies of its reality. It's why I regularly make graphics of my favorite book quotes, interview and feature authors on my website, and film overly excited fangirl segments on YouTube. (Not to mention writing this book!) Every word we read makes an imprint on our minds. Sometimes it's so powerful it impacts our hearts like a hammer to a nail, and other times it's like a graceful and calm waterfall washing over us.

Those words, those stories, dear reader, have *power*.

It is my hope and my personal mission to convey that through each of these letters. May you be inspired to keep writing those words in your heart onto paper (or computer screen). There is a new reader, ready and willing, to embrace those words and fangirl with all his or her heart.

Encouraging You to Dream Big,

Laura A. Grace

Always Rereading

Dear Author,

I thought of you today. I was walking past my bookcase and decided to take a moment to stop and admire all the pretty covers and spines. As my eyes wandered over the shelves, I came across your books and smiled so big because I absolutely *love* your series. It was not only one of the first series to really release my inner fangirl, but even more importantly, it introduced me to you: my favorite author!

Though I'm fairly sure I've already told you, I want you to know this will be my fourth time rereading these books. Yep, my *fourth*! I've been itching to dive back into these characters and am super excited to do so again! Your heroes are absolutely swoonworthy, hilarious, and make me giggle every time I think of them. It doesn't matter how many times I experience their story, they pull me in just as deeply the first time I read. I simply can't get enough of them and your story-world!

If they were real, I would do everything I could to meet them. Goodness, I would do everything I could to meet *you*! I would *love so much* for a chance to meet you in real life (even though I know I would get a little starstruck). It would be a dream come true to physically talk face-to-face. Hopefully, one day I will be able to, but until then, I will eagerly continue to reread this series, gush about it to my friends, and then repeat the process all over again.

>Love to Reread Your Stories,
>
>Your Enthusiastic Fangirl

Character Conversations

Dear Author,

I am all squeals and giggles as I pen this letter because something super fun happened to me recently and *I had* to share it with you.

You know how you share your "character conversations" with us readers? I have always found them to be engaging and sometimes extremely entertaining as you share going back and forth with your character (or characters). Since reading your book and learning even more about your characters, I've caught myself trying to talk to them too, especially the other day!

I was coming home from the grocery store and listening to the car radio when I realized the song playing could *totally* be your heroine's theme song! This got me wondering what she would think of me saying so and if she'd agree or not. That, of course, led to *me* having my *own* mini "character conversation" with her! It made me so, so, so happy and was super cool! (I understand why you share your conversations now. They are so much fun!)

I hope you'll continue sharing conversations with your characters from all your stories with us! I enjoy it immensely and found it to be such a highlight of my day to talk with them too.

Thankful for Magical Moments,

Your Happy Fangirl

Your Debut

Dear Author,

Has anyone told you recently your debut novel is *amazing*? (And I mean super, super, super amazing!) Well, no matter if someone did or didn't, because I want you to know *I* thought it was incredible. When I first got an early copy, I knew an emotional adventure was in store for me, but didn't realize how much of an *emotional* adventure.

From the first chapter, I was completely hooked, and my heart just broke for our heroine. As I kept reading, my heart clenched more and more, but when I got to your hero's story and learned more about his backstory, I was totally done for. I cried quite a bit, but I will tell you when I finished reading your book, I felt immensely encouraged and inspired.

I want to be someone like your hero is. Someone who is brave, bold, and shows others through their actions and words that people are worth fighting for. I want to step out of my "bookish" worlds and enter our "real world" to make a difference in someone's life. I feel I only need to look at the friends, family, and strangers around me to leap into action.

Truly, I don't think there are enough words for me to describe how much your book pushed me to step out of my comfort zone and get involved in others' lives. Thank you for showing me that, dear author. Your book will always hold a special place in my heart, and I pray every time I see it, I'll remember all I shared with you here.

Wanting to Make a Difference,

Your Changed Fangirl

You'll Publish Soon

Dear Author,

How I wish this letter could come packed with hugs! Please know I would be bear-hugging you and squeezing all the love into it I possibly could. I saw you mention you were having to put writing and publishing your book on hold and my heart broke for you.

I can't imagine how hard of a decision that was, but please know it will be okay. I'm unable to say "I promise," but I can assure you us readers, *this* reader, are going to keep supporting you. It doesn't matter if your book is published tomorrow (which would be super awesome) or a year from now. I can say for certain I will continue to cheer you on and "stalk" all your updates.

Based on every snippet you've shared from your upcoming book (and what I've read in your other books), you have this gritty way of writing that reminds me that though the world may be dark, we can look above and still hope. This situation is no different.

One day, you'll publish this new story you've been working hard on, and I'll be right there celebrating with you when you do. Until then, I encourage you to remain hopeful and keep writing and editing. I'm eagerly looking forward to when I can hold your beautiful story in my hands and gush how much I love it.

>Cheering You On,
>
>Your Supportive Fangirl

Thank You

Dear Author,

It's been on my heart to tell you thank you. Truly, thank you for taking the time to share your stories with us readers. You seem to always make time to listen to us fangirls ramble how much we loved about your book and appreciate it so much. I couldn't imagine all the stress and pressure on you to keep up with writing deadlines, raising a family, having a job, and other commitments on top of that. It's amazing that you still have time to chat with us readers!

I'll admit I usually read books as an escape, but seeing all the hard work you do and being so involved with others makes me not want to just escape into a new world. It makes me want to do my part as a reader and share about your work everywhere I can.

I want to show my thanks for you taking the time to pen the stories in your heart by consistently gushing to my reader friends. I want to take pretty book photos and share them with the Bookstagram community. I want to do a fan-made book trailer in hopes of enticing others to pick up your book.

I want to do all the things! I am now making it a personal goal to give back to you by finding creative ways to share all the book love. More readers need to know more about these great stories of yours, and I am going to do my best to let them know!

Ever Yours,

Your Thankful Fangirl

Release Day

Dear Author,

Happy Book Birthday! I'm *so* very excited for you! (And for us fans!) The story you have worked so hard on is now officially out in the world where we readers can devour it. (I know I will be! I ordered the e-book as soon as it was available.) I can only imagine what you must be feeling as I have *eagerly* been looking forward to this day since you started sharing a few excerpts while writing. The more you shared, including your epic cover, the more agony I felt in *not* being able to read it ASAP.

Now all that's changed because I *can* finally read it! I feel like I've been the meme where it says, "Shut up and take my money!" for the past few months. That feeling has only gotten stronger ever since you did the official cover reveal and book description. I just know I am going to love it! How could I not when it contains all the action and all the romance? Those are two of my favorite parts of a good story!

Hopefully today (and this week), you can celebrate in the best and funniest way possible! Maybe a dance party with confetti cannons going off? How about an all-you-can-eat buffet of your favorite desserts? Makes me wish I could attend no matter how you celebrate, but know I'll be celebrating with you from afar and telling other readers your book was published today.

With All the Excitement,

Your Giddy Fangirl

I Can't Cope

Dear Author,

You are so, so, so sneaky! I write that while laughing because I remember you warning us readers to brace ourselves for "all the things" concerning your newest novel. Little did I know how serious I should have taken your words—as being immensely shocked and sorrowful is not what I had in mind.

A friend of mine gave me a magnet that says, "I mourn the death of fictional characters." I am not ashamed to say this has been true for me with every book I've read, but yours especially. My first reaction to your plot twist was absolute shock. I literally stared at the page for a minute and wondered if I really read what I thought I just did. Then I reread it only to realize I *did* read it right! After my shock "faded" (I still don't think I've fully recovered), the tears came, and I did a desperate search for my tissue box. That twist was emotionally heartbreaking!

How am I going to cope when reading your next book in this series? Even though it's been a week since I read that scene, my heart still aches. I think for future reference you should include in the beginning a warning label. I like this: "Warning: Known to emotionally wreck readers. Proceed with tissues." Maybe I'll include it in my next recommendation of your book to reading friends because even though I cried, it was an amazing story and I want other readers to cry with me too (and love this book).

                Stuck in Your Story,

                Your Emotional Fangirl

It's Done?

Dear Author,

I'm wiping tears from my eyes as I write to you because can you believe your series is over? I feel like I can't. I'm still in denial that I won't be having any more late nights with your characters and immersed in your extraordinary world.

The final conclusion was absolutely wonderful! As the series progressed, I knew I loved all your characters (except the bad guy, who I very much did *not* like), but I didn't realize until I read "The End" how much they had grown on me. It was *so* satisfying to see the ending everyone deserved and the quest they worked so hard to fulfill finally completed. It was heart-moving and saddening all at the same time. I just want to continue reading these characters' adventures and cheering them on!

Have you considered writing a follow-up novella? I would love, love, *love* to read more of your fantastic world and stay with your characters even longer. (Just thinking about it makes me excited!) I really am not ready to say goodbye and think you may feel that way too. I truly hope so! Maybe I can help convince you by asking a few other fangirls to share their excited thoughts about this idea (in case you're on the fence if us readers would be interested or not).

Please know we are! I loved this series and already look forward to rereading it again sometime soon.

Not Ready to Say Goodbye

Your Blessed Fangirl

I'm Here for You

Dear Author,

I remember when I first read your book. I was an explosion of emotions page after page. I reached out to you expressing all my feelings on social media through emojis, whole sentences capitalized, and more exclamation and question marks than I knew what to do with. Do you remember? You told me at one point I either needed to order pizza for dinner or put food in the crock pot because the twist was coming. When I got to that part, I cried and promptly told you that you were right.

For the whole story, I was super invested as bad thing after bad thing kept happening to your characters. I cheered, went into a state of shock, got mad at your hero for *still* not kissing the girl, and a jumble of other emotions as I binge read your book within a few days.

Why am I reminding you of my fangirl journey through your book? Because no matter how rough things may get in your writing and publishing journey, I want you to know I am here for you as your reader. I support you. My mission is to read your books, squeal and gush about them to other readers, and then encourage you to keep writing (even if your edits don't save like they did recently). It's my hope if I keep doing so, you'll feel going through hard days like that will be worth it for excited readers like me.

Always Supporting You,

Your Hopeful Fangirl

I'm Not Afraid to Bribe

Dear Author,

Thank you so much for always letting me excitedly ramble to you about your book! There is something so thrilling about chatting with an author while reading and then have them respond with the "inside scoop." It really makes the reading experience very memorable and a personal treasure in my heart. They are some of my favorites because of that reason alone!

With your latest book, it was awesome to release my inner fangirl once again. I have such a blast sharing all my ramblings, especially when the stakes keep getting higher and higher and I feel like I simply can't handle the angst any longer. Not knowing what will happen next is agony. Being able to share my feelings makes it a little bearable, but not by much!

However! If there was a way for me to possibly entice you to share what's about to happen *before* I read those intense parts, then I will have to diligently work to find out what it is. Is it chocolate? Books? Special items of fantasy creatures? You name it, and I'll send it as a thank you (and a little bribery too).

In the meantime, though, I'll continue to keep an eye out for that lucky moment and send you more of my ramblings. I hope they make you laugh and giggle as they do for me!

> Until the Next Book,
>
> Your Excited Fangirl

I See You

Dear Author,

You are such an inspiration! Every time I see you post on social media, I feel so encouraged by your transparency with us readers. I know you're a person just like me, but sometimes I forget that. I admire authors like you *very* much, and seeing you deal with similar struggles reminds me I can overcome them too. Just like you do!

I hope you won't stop sharing your heart and stories with us. I know you recently mentioned that your newest book is not for everyone, but please, don't stop. No matter what "nay-sayers" comment or tell you, the world needs to hear what you have to say. They're words of hope, encouragement, light, truth, and love. All of your books reflect this on a deep and personal level that goes beyond creating an intriguing story world with great characters.

So with release day right around the corner, I want to ultimately share with you the same thing you share with your readers. You are seen and loved. You're not on this journey alone (even if you are the only one writing) because your fangirls will be walking right there with you.

Don't doubt you're making a difference in others' lives. I can assure you that you are just by being the amazing person who inspires, encourages, and supports everyone around them. It's part of why I will always be one of your fangirls and devour your stories.

Thankful for You,

Your Loving Fangirl

Recommending to Everyone

Dear Author,

Can I take a moment to gush about your story? I just finished your book the other day and my heart is overflowing with so much excitement! I'm very, very, *very* thankful my friend recommended it because I would have been missing out on this incredible, heroic tale (which makes me sad just thinking about).

As I started reading, I simply could not keep quiet about your book. I kept gushing to my family at home, in the car, at the store, and wherever else we might be. They *had* to know how much I was *deeply* enjoying it! When I had told them everything I loved about this story, I went online and did the same thing. When friends asked for recommendations, your book was the first one I mentioned. When a bookish question was asked about favorite characters, I made sure to tell them all about yours and then some. I don't want to stop letting people know how good this book is!

Now that I have discovered your work, I will be buying any *and* all of your stories. I am officially now one of your fangirls and refuse to *not* gush about this story if I think a friend or another reader will enjoy it. Even if I'm not sure someone will like it, I'll tell them about it anyway. I'm going to do everything I can to share how much I love this story because I desperately want you and others to know that I'm really hoping you'll continue publishing more books.

      Can't Stop Talking About Your Story,

           Your New Fangirl

Rescue Your Characters

Dear Author,

I absolutely love how creative your stories are! With every new book you release, you seem to blow me away in the fun world-building elements you have and quirky character abilities. Plus, I always end up laughing at some point when I'm reading. I'm so thankful for that! I firmly feel we always need a good laugh—and what better way to do that for a reader than by reading your stories?

Every time I purchase one of your new books, I get a little thrill because I'll be diving into an epic new adventure *and* it will be an adventure like no other. I already know there will be no disappointments ahead, but your characters might not feel the same way. If I could, I would kidnap them and wrap them in bubble wrap to keep them safe! My heart aches for every new character I get attached to because I know they'll get hurt in some way. You're wonderfully mean! You know that, right?

If I could rescue them, they'd no longer have to worry if they will finally reunite with their loved one, or be on the run, or have to fight for their lives. They would be nice and safe in the place of my choosing, and I would *only* think about telling you where they are if you can keep them safe. Please no more hurting them? You want them to be happy too, right?

I hope your answer is "yes" because I fully support keeping your characters happy and protected. Otherwise, I'm breaking out the bubble wrap and searching for your story world's portal!

Wanting to Protect Your Characters,

Your Cautious Fangirl

Thank You

Dear Author,

I've always felt writers are brave people. They take the stories in their heads, write them down, and then publish them with a world of readers hungry for more stories. I can't fathom how intimidating it must be to know a book you poured your heart into could possibly be unappreciated by readers, but how satisfying it must be when a reader *does* love your book *and* see your heart!

Thank you for sharing this story, because I was one of those readers. You took a story and made it so much more. Your characters became *people* who showed me not to be afraid of others who are different than me and own our uniqueness. You've highlighted your series as celebrating just that, and it shines so brightly in your writing. It spurred me to embrace others openly and without fear.

That might have not happened with another story. Yes, I realize there are probably *a lot* of books that could convey this, but *your* book was the one that touched me. I'm already looking forward to reading more in this series because I know I'll be touched again. I don't believe it will be a one-time deal, as you have something beautiful in this series. I know it's going to affect plenty of others the same way it did me.

> Positively Affected by Your Stories,
>
> Your Touched Fangirl

Please Be You

Dear Author,

I was thinking of you today when I bought a new book. As I browsed the books offered at my local book store, I wanted to tell you that though there are hundreds of thousands of authors in the world, there is only *one* you. One incredible, amazing, imaginative *you*.

That idea excites me as a reader, because I know every time I order one of your books, I will always get something uniquely different because only you can share it. There might be stories that have similar themes or messages, but the heart of the story will be your beautiful heart. That's so awesome! To me, that means you never have to worry if your books are as good as another author's because they *are* that good. You don't even need to worry if you're a "successful" author because you were from the very first time you signed a contract with a publisher or published your book yourself.

You, dear author, never have to change your writing or your stories. You offer readers a special kind of magic only your fingers can create, and your books leave a special, one-of-a-kind touch only found in them. Please never, ever, ever underestimate the power of your stories because I know I *never* underestimate the emotional impact your stories will have on me.

Always Here to Encourage,

Your Passionate Fangirl

Acknowledgements

This book came from a place of love and God-given bravery. *Dear Author* truly wouldn't even be in readers' hands if it had not been for a myriad of people, including:

My Heavenly Father: thank you for loving me and blessing me with this strong passion to help authors. You inspired these words during a dark period in my life and have never left me or forsaken me.

My family, especially my husband: thank you for hearing all my joys, fears, and frustrations as well as celebrating this whole journey with me. I've told you before, and I will tell you again; I'm pursuing writing because you all believed in me even when I didn't believe in myself.

Neko Inklings: thank you for encouraging me, supporting me, and telling me not to give up. I know this book is not a manga, but you ladies have been so involved in seeing this book become a reality. It means so much, and I'm thankful I get to call you ladies friends. (Maybe one day I'll beat you in watching a new anime and gushing first. Or maybe just keeping up with the new anime in general. Or better yet, maybe just watching that last season of *Voltron: Legendary Defender*. Ha!)

Realm Mothers: you are some of the most inspiring women I know! Thank you for answering all my writing and publishing questions as well as praying for me. Thank you for simply *being* there. I'm thankful you ladies are a safe place for anything and everything. Cheering you each on and praying for you!

Hannah S.J. Williams: thank you for these incredible illustrations! I smile and laugh every time I see them because they are better than what I imagined. You helped bring this book to life and made it "pop" the way I prayed it would. Thank you!

Veronica Lynn, Angie Grigaliunas, H. A. Titus, and Savannah Jezowski: thank you, ladies, so much for helping bring this story into the world with your editing, proofreading, and answers to my questions about formatting (and formatting my page numbers). Thank you for not shying away from all my questions, sharing ideas, and being patient with me during each step of this process. I am blessed to have worked with you!

My precious beta readers: thank you. Those two words do not convey how much your glowing feedback meant to me. When I said, "I quit," your words told me, "*Don't.*" You reminded me that this book has a place in the world and that it can encourage authors like I hoped and prayed it would. This book is here because you helped get it here. From the bottom of my heart, thank you.

My fellow Unicorn Questers: you guys are amazing, and I am tremendously thankful for you! Your excitement has been so contagious, and it is absolutely thrilling to have you by my side. As a new author, I understand when other authors say it takes a community to share a book. It's true, and you guys have been a bright, glittery light of awesomeness on my journey. Thank you! (Can't wait to share my manga next with you, Questers!)

Cathy Hinkle: I love you, friend, and appreciate you encouraging me to publish this book (and telling me to be prepared to sell it at Realm Makers!). You're amazing, and I can't wait to read your book one day!

Haruichi Furudate, (manga creator of *Haikyu!!*): thank you for publishing Hinata's story. Though you may never see this, his journey of embracing and being proud of his role as well as his growing friendship with Kageyama had a profound effect on me and my writing journey. I'm thankful I was able to watch some of the anime and read part of the manga while editing this book because it helped me get where I am today. (Also, thank you Beka Grimikova for recommending this anime and manga to me! I will forever be grateful, friend.)

The countless people who have been on this magical quest with me: thank you. So many people, especially authors, have been involved in my life that encouraged me to keep writing, keep trying, and never give up. There were friends who prayed for me when I didn't know what to pray, poured words of hope into my weary heart, and stood beside me while I cried from wondering if I would ever publish. Truly, you have impacted my life in life-altering ways and deeply blessed because of you. I didn't think I could ever be a writer or even an author, but you helped me see otherwise. Thank you.

Lastly, but certainly not least, thank you, Jesus. For everything.

About the Author

Laura A. Grace had a lifelong dream of getting to know authors behind the covers of her favorite reads. Little did she know that one day she would become an author too! Now an avid book blogger at Unicorn Quester and writer of clean, Christian manga, Laura creatively balances her passions of supporting indie authors and feeding her readers new stories. In between, she wields plastic lightsabers with her children and binge-watches anime with her husband. Join her quest to find wandering unicorns for your favorite authors at unicornquester.com!

Visit Laura online at unicornquester.com
Facebook: UQ4authors
Twitter: @UQ4authors
Instagram: @UQ4authors
YouTube: Laura A. Grace

Connect with Laura

Laura loves connecting with authors and readers alike! Want to say hello, subscribe to her newsletter, or squeal over an upcoming book release? Connect with her at her website or on social media!

www.unicornquester.com
Facebook: UQ4authors
Twitter: @UQ4authors
Instagram: @UQ4authors
YouTube: Laura A. Grace

Email Newsletter: www.unicornquester.com/newsletter

CPSIA information can be obtained
at www.ICGtesting.com
Printed in the USA
FSHW011407081219
64688FS

9 781733 376808

Think your words might not matter?

Think again.

Words have the power to change lives, especially when they are used to create meaningful stories. In this collection of letters, bookish fangirl Laura A. Grace addresses topics related to every writer's journey. From "character conversations," to embracing one's unique writing style, to celebrating a release day—there is a letter for every author no matter where they may be in sharing their story with others.

"Dear Author" includes six illustrations by Hannah S.J. Williams.